Gilbert and Me

Original Paintings by
ANN M. RIGGOTT

Verse by Gladys Jenkins Riggott

With love and joy this book is dedicated to
Christian Guy Timm Jurgensen
and to
Emily, Dylan, Grace, Kyle and Jacob

"AND HE TOOK THE CHILDREN IN HIS ARMS,
PUT HIS HANDS ON THEM AND BLESSED THEM."
Mark 10:16

Original paintings in this book are also available as open or limited edition prints. For information on purchasing a print call: 1-507-286-8727

ACKNOWLEDGEMENTS

Special thanks and appreciation to the following people for their help with this project: Dean Riggott, Jennifer Jurgensen, Don and Kathy Riggott, Gayle Timm

CREDITS

Original Paintings: Ann Riggott
Verse: Gladys Riggott
Design & Layout: Ann Riggott, Sean McDonald
Printing: Doosan Printing, Seoul, Korea

ISBN # 0-9777641-0-9
First Edition / Hard Cover / $16.95
Library of Congress Catalog Number: 2006901532

All rights reserved. No part of this publication may be reproduced or used in any form by any means — graphics, electronic, or mechanical, including framing, photocopying, recording, taping, nor any information storage and retrieval system — without prior written permission from the publisher.

Copyright © 2006 Riggott Studio of Fine Art

PUBLISHED BY

Riggott Studio of Fine Art
321 14th St N.E.
Rochester, MN 55906
Phone: 507-286-8727
riggottart@yahoo.com

My name's Christian, and I am two.
I have so many things to do.
My papa's farm is so much fun,
with lots of room to play and run.
There are cats, cows, and chickens too.
And three puppies that are brand new.
So turn the pages one by one.
See all the things that I have done.

My best friend is Gilbert my cat,
who doesn't have to wear a hat.
He follows me wherever I go,
and has soft fur. I love him so.

They're black and white
    and they say moo –
But tell me, please,
    what do they do?

I put my boots and raincoat on
and found a puddle on the lawn.
Splishy, splash – oh, what a sight.
I'm so glad it rained last night.

Chickens in their fluffy feathers
    think it's time to eat.
I'll get some sweet cornmeal
    to give them as a treat.

Chickens are fed and now, you see,
geese have gathered round Zachary.
He doesn't know quite what to do,
but Mom says he can feed them too.

It's time for Megan to go to school,
but doing chores first, is the rule.
She gathers eggs so Mom can make,
some cookies and a yummy cake.

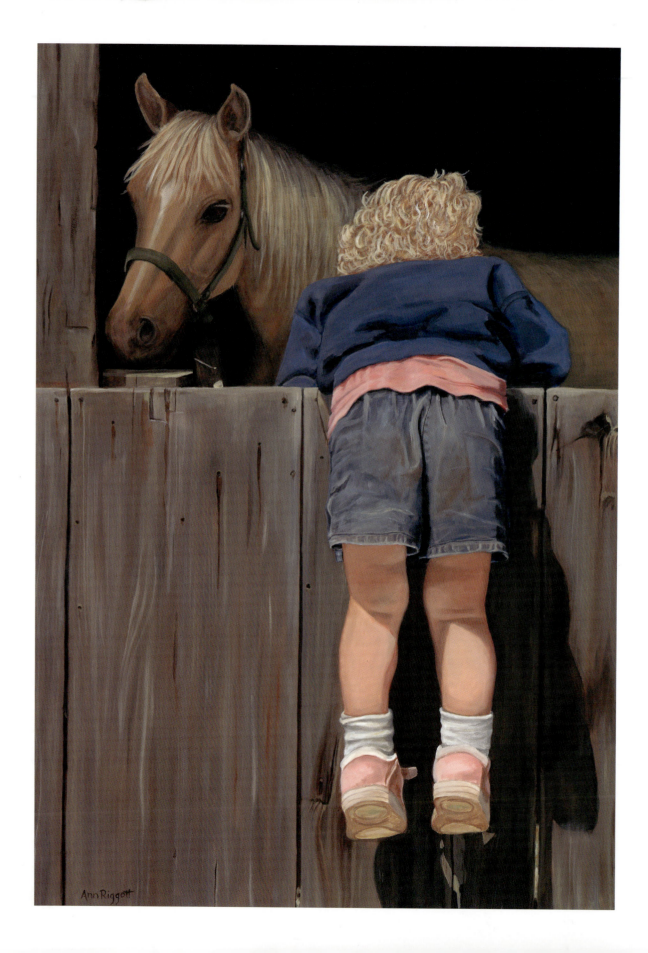

We visit Nellie every day
to make sure that she has her hay.
We're going on a buggy ride,
with Grammy sitting by my side.

This is my sister, Emily.
She's as bossy as can be.
All dressed up in Sunday clothes,
she says, "Kitty, don't bite my toes!"

My cousin Dylan comes to stay
and teases kitties in his way.
He's full of pep and energy,
and always wants to follow me.

I found my new straw hat and pole,
and ran down to the fishing hole.
Now, little fishy in the brook,
come and get my wormy hook.

Gracie dressed and combed her hair,
then ran out to the meadow fair.
The sun is shining in the sky,
as woolly sheep pass slowly by.

As Dean went for a walk, he saw three puppies playing in the straw. When he sat down, they tried to chew his bright blue coat and his left shoe.

My snowman stands there big and tall,
    and just stares back at me.
I really like his coat and hat,
    but he has no feet, you see.

Stars and moon are overhead,
dark has come, it's time for bed.
I'll rock my friendly bear to sleep,
and pray the Lord my soul to keep.